It's Impossible from Scratch! Or Is It?

A Successful Business Start-up Guide

Preface

I needed this book when I started out ranching. Even though I grew up ranching, when I took over management at age 23, I had no idea how to create a cash flow budget, how to read a financial statement or estimate the stocking rate of a property. I had never even written a ranch business check. I could pull a calf, sew up a prolapse, irrigate and do most of the tactical aspects of ranching reasonably well, but when it came to running the business, I had a lot to learn. It was a baptism of fire. My father and mother accepted a call to serve as service missionaries in Mexico and left me in charge of the ranch. My wife and I had just had our 1st child and we eagerly accepted the challenge. Both of us loved ranching.

Dad had put in place systems that made up for my incompetency and lack of experience. All I had to do was not screw it up- pay the bills, brand the calves, put up the hay, wean the calves… repeat. My parents came home from their mission to find the place in relatively good condition so they signed up to go on another mission leaving my wife and me with our growing family again in charge of the ranch. They served five missions throughout the world.

There we days that I longed to have my father back at home as I faced the challenges of operating a large cow-calf operation. The ranch employed up to six employees with three different locations spread out over many miles. The pressure of being responsible for not only my family, but our employees and their families, managing the finances, dealing with government agencies and our dependence on operating debt weighed heavily on me. Much of the romance of ranching had faded away. I needed a mentor. The student was ready and the teachers began to appear.

I was blessed to meet and learn from some wonderful people. Dave Pratt, Bud Williams and Fred Provenza were a few of the original people who helped to open my mind to a more holistic way of ranch management. My wife and I left college to come back to the ranch. For many years I did not think I needed to further my education. As I began to learn, I developed an insatiable desire to continue to learn and I strived to apply what I learned on our operation. Between missions my parents questioned the different path that we were taking the ranch, but supported us in most of the decisions we made. Neighbors began to question our sanity, and one even bet my brother in law that we would be broke within a few years!

Valuable perspective was gained as I began to network with fellow ranchers from north and south America. The challenges of ranching did not go away; in fact in many ways they increased. The more I learned, the more I realized that I was responsible for the success or failure of the business. I could no longer find excuses and blame the outcome on the weather, the government or even the market. It became apparent that what some ranchers saw as a challenge, others recognized as an opportunity and prospered because of it. I am grateful for the great people that I have been blessed to work with, learn from and be influenced by.

Aron Hansen is one of the people that has come to our ranch. He too shares the insatiable desire to learn and live true principles. I am grateful that he has the courage to share his experience and knowledge in this book. Wise people learn from the experience of others and this book will definitely increase the reader's wisdom.

Jared-Nevada

Introduction

      The cowboy is the greatest American hero. Most young boys at one time or another dream of being a cowboy when they grow up. He represents all the morals and ethics that we all admire. He brings us to a place in our minds of someone we can relate and look up to.

      But a cowboy to a young man can mean many things to an adult who has more wherewithal and discernment, what is a cowboy? Is he a rancher, a rodeo star, a farmer, or the romantice rider of the wide open spaces that hollywood has portrayed? There is a fundamental difference between all of these. Each of these job descriptions is very different and all require a lot of knowledge and skill. The romantic figure on the big screen unfortunately doesn't exist. A rancher or farmer is fundamentally a producer of food and fiber for the world. Producing food and fiber for the world is in the industry of production agriculture and it is the most amazing industry on earth. Producing food and fiber doesn't have the romance of the rodeo, and it requires different skills. A rodeo star is a professional athlete, they spend their time training or competing. Not to take anything away from our rodeo hero's, but production agriculture takes different skills and areas of focus. Producing food and fiber for the world is a bit more work, and a bit less romantic than the stereotype that we "cowboys" are labeled with. Agriculture the oldest industry in history. It is also the most recession-proof industry. As long as people still need to eat, we'll always have a job. That doesn't mean that times can't get hard but, it does mean is that our products will always be in demand. While farmers concentrate on growing products from the soil, ranchers spend their energies producing products from animals.

Ranching historically has been hard, never-ending work. The experience of children who grow up on farms and ranches is that the work never ends. The long hot or cold days that go on and on. They see the ranch become less and less productive over time. They watch the financial stress on their parents. They hear their parents' conversations with each other and the neighbors about how hard it is.

The parents may even discourage the children from ever choosing a career in agriculture. Not surprisingly, after the child has graduated they never seem to return to the ranch.

Ranching doesn't have to be an "all go no quit" type of business. It can be quite enjoyable and rewarding(not to say there isn't work.) The inherent nature of the livestock business requires persistence and a strong work ethic. You are on call twenty-four hours a day seven days a week. But if you love the work you are doing it is not work at all.

There are those of us who are not turned off by the hard work or the uncertainty of ranching. Some who would love the opportunity to take over their family's ranch, find themselves in the wrong family. Their families do not own a ranch. And so they embark on the journey to start their own. Others find themselves suddenly responsible for the family operation. While yet others choose neither and choose to work as buckaroos, cow punchers, and ranch hands who think it's only a dream to be able to own a ranch someday.

The enterprising would-be-ranchers may then become awestruck as they learn how much capital they will need to start their ranch. Among aspiring ranchers, there is always talk of how much is stacked against them. They will need hundreds of thousands, or even millions of dollars to reach a point where they can get into ranching at a level that they feel that they can make a living. There are real estate challenges, there are climatic obstacles, as well as a whole host of other adversaries to overcome

There are those with the desire to run a ranch, but not the skills required. The skills needed to run a ranch profitably and adequately are different than the skills necessary to work on a ranch. Someone may be the best cowboy on the crew, but that does not mean that he is qualified to run the ranch. The best bronc stomper or roper may not have the skills to keep the cost of gain down on a set of cattle. The ranch owner/operator must have both sets of skills to keep the production of the livestock at an acceptable level as well as keeping a pulse on the bottom line while creating a sustainable business that will thrive on the natural resource for generations to come.

High production in livestock does not guarantee a profit. I have seen many examples where there is high production and losing money. So the more productive they are the less they make or the more they lose. The aspiring ranchers, who have both the cowboy skills and the production management skills and who have some vague plan as to how they can acquire the necessary capital, still might not know how to ensure a profitable business.

These are only some of the challenges I faced while I was pursuing my dream. You will get the answers to these problems and much more from reading this book to completion. This book is not meant to be an exhaustive study of the art and science of producing food and fiber (which is to say, agriculture). There are many books on the husbandry skills that are essential to your success in starting and maintaining a ranch business of your own. This is a book of what you have to know, and who you have to be to achieve success as a rancher, not so much how to do specific tasks. This book is meant to answer the questions that you don't yet know enough to ask.

Through my journey, I have learned what skills are important, and which are not (what is not important will surprise you as much as what is). This book will give you all the tools you will need to get from where you are to where you want to be. I will teach you the philosophy and the secrets to creating the future you want- as a successful rancher..

Follow your dreams, or you'll work for someone who did.

Chapter 1: Daydreams

Whatever the mind of man can conceive and bring himself to believe he can achieve- Napoleon Hill

I grew up a town kid. Both of my parents came from small family farm backgrounds; I was not as lucky. My parents' sheep and cow operation were casualties of the farm crisis in the 1980's I spent most of my childhood in Utah with my mother; but when I was 13 I moved with my father in Nevada. My parents divorced when I was quite young, both remarried and had other families.

During those years in Utah, I watched any western movie that I could. I related to the cowboys- like John Wayne's characters, and "The Man From Snowy River." I loved acting them out. I played the leading roles in movies I'd seen, as well as those that I made up. I also had any cowboy toy I could get my hands on. The books I checked out of the school library were all cowboy related. In school, all the kids called me "cowboy Jim," I'm sure they got tired of my imagination's focus. So you could say that my childhood was spent in the "wild west," at least in my imagination. My cowboy daydreams didn't stop me from having friends or playing some video games or basketball or baseball or all the normal things. But whenever my mind was free to drift it reverted to "cowboy stuff." I dreamed of all the experiences and adventures I would have someday.

My extended family all still had farms or some type of livestock operation. I watched as my cousins grew up in the life I wanted. It bothered me that most of them didn't enjoy it. They took for granted what experiences they fortunate enough to have. I would visit from time to time and try to soak up as much of it as I could, to learn anything I could because I knew I would need it eventually. My father would pick me up for his scheduled visitations and take me to my grandparents' farm. It was quite small, maybe a few hundred acres, with a hundred ewes, and no more than a handful of cows. But it was the 'true west' to me. It nurtured my obsession. I loved helping with the work to be done, whether it was lambing or shearing or moving a few cows around. There was always a horse to ride or a dirt bike to explore on. Because it was also my grandparents' house, it was always the most fun place to be, with very little, if any, reprimand- it was just the best. I looked forward to going there.

Even though I loved it, no one ever encouraged me to pursue agriculture as a profession. The mantra of "you can't make money in agriculture" was drummed into me. The idea that you had to have a job so you could have a hobby farm was what they lived and believed so therefore what they preached to me.

At the age of 13, I had moved in with my father who worked as a gold miner in the mines in Nevada. His work schedule was horrendous. I don't know how people do that type of work with an even worse schedule. Alternating days and nights with various days off. It pays good, but it's just not for me let's put it that way. But some people don't love "cowboy stuff," but maybe they love "playing in the dirt." As long as someone enjoys what they do I think that's great. We all must choose our own path. Be sure you don't regret the path you've chosen.

We always had horses around, though not all of them were safe enough for how green I was. He was a backyard breeder of some quite good horses. He would buy quality papered genetics to continually upgrade his mares. He would only get a colt or two from each mare; then he had fresh genetics, so he moved on to improve them. So we always had at least one stud around, and several mares with several more colts. A 'broke' horse didn't seem to have that much value to my father. I know this because whenever something got 'broke' enough that we could ride without incident, it seems that it was sold shortly after, just to buy some 'un-broke' something or other. I didn't understand what his objectives were. I understand them a little more now.

So my horse education was primarily on colts that were learning just like I was. My father had the right balance of experience and courage, he was starting colts clear past 60 years of age. Though I was a strapping young man when I first moved there, I had had minimal experience. I got myself into a few wrecks, nothing severe, but enough to start to understand the power that animals have and to give them the appropriate respect. But I had to learn on the job, so to speak. My father wasn't very patient, he could be quick-tempered and demanding.

Aside from the horse experience I gained from my father, my decision to move with him rather than stay in Utah allowed me broader experiences. My older sister's husband, Kelly, had family with a ranch just a few hours away. I loved to go out there. They had regular cattle drives to and from summer and winter ranges. I also got to experience jobs like calving heifers, branding, doctoring sick calves, weaning, etc. I loved it I thought that I had reached the top - I mean how could it get any better? I loved to ride, and also didn't mind any other chores like fencing or irrigating. I spent many weekends, spring breaks, and even a summer or two there. It changed my life, and shaped its direction in more ways than one. I was very fortunate to have those experiences. If it wasn't for the time I spent and experience I gained there, I don't think I would've ever considered that I could actually become a cowboy or a rancher.

During this period, life also dealt me one of the hardest blows to my belief that my ranching dreams were possible. I was probably 14 years old, and when around town at the grocery store or the gas station, I would pick up the free real estate listing papers. I would get them every chance I could and flip right to the ranch section. I would study, and dream, and drool about buying one of the properties. I would find on a map where they were, and any "for sale" signs around that we'd drive past always caught my eye. I would dream about this valley, or that hillside, and how it would be to start a ranch from the ground up. I knew that I had to acquire land first, then animals could come later.

At this time I wasn't working yet, but I knew that in a few years I would be getting my driver's license, and then I would be able to get a job and start saving for my ranch. I remember doing the math on this one particular property that had been for sale for quite a while. I had kept tabs on it every time I picked up the latest real estate magazine. This property wasn't large, but it was huge in price. It was listed for one million five hundred thousand dollars. I knew I could get a job for around six or seven dollars per hour. So I got excited, thinking I can just save up enough to get it. Then I did the math on how long it would take me to save up that much money. After the math was completed, only one word would describe how I felt, devastated. It would be over a hundred years before I would have saved that much. I thought it was impossible. But then a solution dawned on me, I wouldn't work for that low of wage my entire life. I could learn more skills and get paid more so it wouldn't take me as long. I speculated that my father was making around twenty dollars an hour, so I did that math, and I also subtracted some living money while I saved. So with some fresh optimism, I set out to recalculate. I figured I could save around twenty-thousand dollars per year. I remember getting ready to push the equals sign with great anticipation and excitement, because I had solved my previous problem, and that I would work for just a few years, then live happily ever after. Sure it would be a few years of hard work, but it would be worth it. So I pushed the equals sign and … I think it was like 75 years or something. I felt like someone kicked me in the stomach. I knew that I didn't want to start ranching at age 75. I had already invested years into this dream, just to have it crushed. It was impossible; I had no more breakthrough solutions to my problem. But I could revert to my fantasy world until I could figure something out. I don't think I believed a solution would present itself. So here I was washed up at 14. I mean dreams don't come true, not for blue-collar workers like us.

I thought maybe I could get some advice from my father, after all, he must know some things that I don't. After visiting with my father about this experience, there were the same old sayings of 'ranching is no way to make a living'. So ranching just turned into a pipe dream for me. I still loved going to help my sister and Kelly, but never really thought it could happen. After all, this is the information age. The only path I could figure it would be possible was to get rich first then I could live my dream. Little did I realize, but I would waste the next 20 years or so chasing pots of gold at the end of rainbows with no real results to show for it. A lot of expensive education but nothing material realized from my efforts.

Returning to life's realities, and deciding I needed a career, I decided to study to be a diesel mechanic. But even while attending college and studying to be a diesel mechanic, of course, in the back of my head I knew the goal was to make significant money so I could buy a ranch someday. The college I was attending was starting a new agriculture program. I knew the administrator, and so I switched majors. I thought there are thousands of jobs within agriculture, surely I could get a degree and make as much money or more, and at least it would be in the industry I wanted. I resisted just going to get a job on a ranch, because I knew that at that low pay it would never be possible to buy a place of my own. So began my college journey.

I had been attending classes for a year and a half or so when an opportunity showed up that forever changed my life. It was possible for us as students to earn ag credits for going to outside ag seminars and doing a report after we'd attended. I thought this was good for me, as I was growing tired of college. I went to several small ones, but soon found a seminar that was put on at Utah State University. The workshop was a week-long class of 8 hours a day, and I could gain a massive number of ag credits if I attended, so I jumped at the chance.

Also in attendance at this class was a couple who managed a ranch in Oklahoma. We hit it right off, and my life would never be the same after. During the seminar, I spent much of my time trying to have side conversations with this couple. Some of the concepts the husband would talk about led me to believe that it was possible to start with nothing and end up with a ranch. He was talking about very foreign concepts than the college professors that had been teaching me about high input ranching and making money three years out of ten. Three years out of ten is how many years the average cow/calf producer shows a profit. I didn't have the right questions there to ask, but it started me on a journey searching for answers.

I got his contact information and kept in contact with him. This led to many paradigm shifts. I asked him many silly questions, enough that he invited me to come to Oklahoma to see him and his operation. I made several trips to spend time with him and learn from him and those he learned from. Here was a guy doing almost exactly opposite of what my college professors were teaching, and he was a successful and happy rancher. He didn't work himself or his employees to death. It seemed like a very productive and happy life. I knew I wanted what he had.

He opened up my mind back to possible again, instead of impossible. You see I had spent almost ten years at this point telling myself that owning my ranch was impossible and that it could never happen for me. I will always be grateful to him for opening the door to possibility. He sent me to some workshops, and advised other classes and workshops I should attend and mentors I should contact. He didn't know it, but during this time I would work at whatever jobs I could and save just enough to go to the next school or to get to go back there to spend time more with him. Here was a guy that had what I wanted, and he knew something I didn't, but I wanted to. I just couldn't get enough. I would come home so optimistic and confident. I loved that feeling.

Chapter 2: What Business Are We In?

Finally, brethren, whatsoever things are true, whatsoever things are honest, whatsoever things are just, whatsoever things are pure, whatsoever things are lovely, whatsoever things are of good report; if there be any virtue, and if there be any praise, think on these things.- Philippians 4:8

Within our worldwide marketplace, there are thousands of businesses. If you break them down, there are only three types. First, there are commodity producers who grow or mine raw materials. Second, there are product businesses who take a raw material commodity and upgrade it somehow into a more usable form. Thirdly, there are service businesses, who do just what their name implies, they provide a service. When I speak about commodities I am talking about the same commodities that are traded on the futures markets, but I am speaking of the cash trade of these raw materials. What the board is doing in Chicago is irrelevant to what I am talking about here.

Many businesses encompass more than one type. An example would be a restaurant: it buys raw food, then upgrades it into serveable food, and then serves it to you. So they are all three. Each business type has different natural inherent laws that must be adhered to be successful. For example in a service business, if you don't serve your customer well enough it doesn't matter how good your product is, they won't buy from you. Or they may purchase once, but they will never be back.

In both the product or service business, discounts are expected for volume purchases. The reverse is true for commodities, the more of a uniform commodity you have, the more it is worth per unit. The fewer items you sell, the less you get for each unit. Here is an example: If you go to the store and buy a bottle of syrup you would pay full retail price. But, if you bought a pallet of the same syrup, or an entire truckload, your cost per item would go down immensely. However, if you buy one red steer, you'll only pay so much for him. But, if you can buy a truckload of red steers that are all uniform you will pay more per steer than if you had just bought the one. To take it even farther, if you were to buy ten truckloads of the same red steers, you would expect to pay even more for each steer. The pricing structure for consumer goods has a different paradigm than the cash commodity market.

Price points for commodities are always fluctuating up and down with each new piece of news affecting the price. Commodity prices are continually trying to balance at the break-even cost of the average producer of that commodity. The price will go up and down, never actually leveling out at the break-even price, because it never can. The price rises because more people are getting in, then the price goes down because more people are selling than buying. Again we're not talking about the futures trading, we're talking about the cash trade. The average cattle producer makes 3% net profit. The *average* producer makes that much, that means for everyone making 4% someone is earning 2% for everyone making 9% someone is losing 6%. The average is the good, the bad, and the ugly all mixed together then divided equally.

The fact is that in a commodity business we are 'price takers'. As 'price takers,' we can do nothing to influence the market. We take what the market will give us. A harsh fact maybe, but it is a fact indeed. Now, I realize we can direct market some animals straight to the consumer, but we can only sell a certain amount at a premium. Any time any volume starts hitting that market, there is not enough demand to support the premium price. Because the price is always trying to balance at a break-even, the only way to stay profitable is to be one of the lowest cost producers in any commodity. I know some cow/calf ranches who spend upwards of seven-hundred-dollars, per-cow, per-year, I also know of some that are less than three hundred. So the dumb question is: who is making the most, and who can stay in business longer, who will survive? Duh! The lowest cost producers. So, if you don't like the idea of prudent management, perhaps the commodity market is not the right one for you. A niche market, or an industry support business might be better suited to you.

Supply Chain

There are several steps that cattle go through before they end up on the table. The cow/calf producer owns calf factories (cows), and each year they sell the calf crop into the market. Next, someone will buy the calf and run it through its yearling year until it weighs seven to eight-hundred pounds. Then, typically, the yearling will go to the feedlot, where it is "finished" and weighs twelve to fourteen-hundred pounds. After harvesting, the beef gets boxed up, then sold to a beef wholesaler, who will then sell it to grocery stores or restaurants. The supply chain I just described is an oversimplification of the process, but this is the bare bones of our industry. There are numerous ways to do each step, and some people own the animal from birth to the plate. But the majority of cattle in the country go through this step-by-step process.

The question for you is what business segment fits you the best. This requires a lot of thought and self-reflection. The cow/calf business is a good business, but it can be a little slow. You work all year for one turn of your inventory per year. The yearling business is a bit busier, but has its own set of challenges. Maybe owning a feedlot that custom feeds for others or your cattle is what would be best. I'm not here to tell you what part of the industry to get involved in. That question is for you to answer for yourself.

Regional and Cultural Differences

Not all pastures or ranches are created equal. Conditions in one place can be different from a place a mile down the road. That is one of the reasons I love ranching. Natural resource management is so complex and has so many variables, and we control almost none of them, like the weather or the market. If your place is high up in the mountains that have snow most of the year, you probably shouldn't be in the cow/calf business because you will be feeding expensive hay most of the year. If your pastures are steep and brushy areas, maybe goats would make the most sense. It is more cost effective to match the animal to the natural conditions than it is to make the ground match what animal you want to run. It is always possible, but will be extremely expensive. Try to take a completely unbiased look at your current condition and decide what animals make the most sense for you to be involved in from your natural resource standpoint. If what your ground will support is not what you want to run, maybe you should find another place that meets the requirements that your animals and will be sustainable. You need to get the right natural resources for what you want to do or get the animal that fits what you have.

Most commodity businesses, but not all, require large tracts of land as their primary natural resource. Land acquisition can be a stumbling block to someone just starting out. The cost of these properties can be incredibly high. Real estate today isn't priced based solely on what it can produce. Other factors are adding to the value of the land - not only based on food and fiber productions- but the alternative uses for anyone else interested in buying it. For instance, aesthetics, if this tract of property is in a position to acquire the urban sprawl of the nearby city, or would make an excellent golf course. Many factors go into the purchase value of land. We will go into some strategies to overcome the land issues in a few chapters, so keep reading.

What business are we as ranchers really in?

You might say " well, of course, we're in the beef business." I would challenge you that the meat packer is in the beef business. Maybe you finish cattle out; I would still suggest you're still not in the beef business you are in the cattle business. It isn't beef until it's on the rail. If you sell anything on the rail, be it cull cows or fat cattle, I guess I would concede you are in the beef business, but you are still producing cattle first. Until it's meat, it's an animal.

You might also say "we sell calves" or "we are in the yearling business." Those might all be true statements, however, if you are growing cattle how do you do it? "Ah ha!" you say "we convert forage into money." Because we take forage and run it through an animal, then we convert the animal into money. Yes, we are getting warmer. Now take it one more step with me.

I would say we are in the solar business. That's right, I said the solar business. Sunlight is hitting your pasture almost every day. Your field is mixing sunlight and soil nutrients to grow grass. The grass is then put through the animal to which is then converted into money. By understanding the entire picture, you can better manage any single one of the variables better.

Try always to think as holistically as you can. You will end up making much more sound decisions.

Chapter 3: The Dealer Deals

Smile and mean it.- Bud Williams

In any business, you have challenges and advantages. In this chapter, we will be talking about those advantages that you possess. I will be referring to them as our 'inventory'. Now, inventories aren't just products that you have stocked up that are for sale. Inventories are anything you can use. It can be a bucket of bolts in the shop that you use, so you don't have to run to the store, it could also be your good credit to get a big loan somewhere. Your inventory is any and every advantage you can utilize.

The Inherent Inventories (Time & Skills):

You have an inventory of time. How well are you using that? We all only have twenty-four hours in a day. No one gets anymore, and no one gets any less. You can't save some of today's time and use it next week. You can't borrow time from tomorrow. Time is running and is going by second-by-second. You can't manage time. Trying to manage time is like trying to manage gravity. You can't, it's a constant law of nature. But what you can do is manage your priorities. Time management is a myth.

But, priority management is how you can control how you spend your time.

You must choose moment by moment what the most important thing you should be doing is. If that is digging a post hole with a bar and shovel then so be it. Or, are you digging this post hole the hard way instead of doing something that can serve you better for longer. In the book "the one thing" by Gary Keller, which I highly recommend, the author tells us to ask ourselves a fundamental question. He starts by telling us to in our mind think about a goal, or a task, or a problem, or a series of them. Now ask yourself, "What is the one thing I can do that will make this thing you're thinking about easier or not necessary at all?" If you are always doing the most important thing you can, the small tasks will take care of themselves.

You have advantages that no one else in the world has. I'm going to call this inventory "yourself." I want you to switch your mind from all the challenges and problems that face you. You do this by changing the questions you are asking yourself. Instead of asking what challenges do I need to overcome? Instead of allowing the dialogue to run in the back of your head; of "It's so hard" or "It'll never work." Or even the question to your subconscious- "What is the next problem I must solve?", to which you'll get an answer very quickly, more and more problems to solve. Ask better questions. For example, "What advantages do I have?" or "How could it work?".

I want you to find your unfair advantages that only you have. These are advantages that only you possess, you have some, and so does everyone else. If you can't find an edge, then keep asking yourself different questions until you figure them out. Through the remainder of our journey together in this book, you need to keep in mind the skills you have. We will be building on those to create a plan that is tailored specifically to you. Maybe you have a high level of expertise when it comes to de-stressing cattle. Or perhaps you're a people person and can verbally communicate well. Whatever your strengths are, make sure you keep them in your mind as what you should be using. Play to your strengths, while always trying to improve your weaknesses. A professional football player doesn't spend all his time working on his baseball swing so that he can work on one of his faults. He works on his football skills. Your skills are the only thing you can rely on when you get in tight situations. Your strengths are what you are good at, and what will end up working for you in the end.

The Traditional Inventories (Money, Feed, Livestock):

In the livestock business, we have three main types of more traditional inventories money/capital, grass/feed/land, and livestock.

Money

The way you manage your money or working capital is probably the highest priority when it comes to managing your livestock business. You can run short of anything else, and fix it generally, with your skills and money combined. Skills, without the money to back it, is unrealizable potential. It's wasted potential.

All agricultural commodity businesses are massively capital and skill intensive. It takes thousands of hours of skill building even to become average. It can also require a truckload of money depending on the size of the operation. This money can come in many forms. It can be in cash, or credit. It can come in the form of trade or leasing opportunities. You can lease a million dollars worth of value for less than it could be purchased. So you don't have to have all the cash in the world to get started. You don't have to have the best credit on the planet. You do have to be creative and never quit trying. Attack any problem from every angle you can think of. If one plan doesn't work, just regroup and attack again.

Credit management is another crucial topic. I would like you to think about this statement. If someone goes broke or is bankrupt or has financial difficulties, do you think they got that way by handling cash or credit? Obviously, they didn't have a lot of cash that was theirs to spend- those difficulties arose from improper use of credit. Using credit imprudently can be the only reason your business fails. You can have everything else dialed in and just right, but the debtor is a slave to the lender. It would be better to grow slower and more organically than to leverage yourself so far that your house of cards comes tumbling down. That being said, credit and leverage can be tools in our toolbox to help us get down the road faster. Please use extreme caution and wisdom when dealing with credit. One of the biggest things is to learn the rules of the credit game before you start playing. The more education and skills that you have on any given subject lowers the risk.

Never run out of money. Nothing will kill a business faster. Cashflow is the lifeblood of a company. A business breaking even with high cash flow will last longer than a business making big profits but can't fulfill their near-term obligations. Cash flow is king. Keep it moving. I'm sure you've all shopped at a superstore before. You know, those places you can buy groceries, furniture, and get your oil changed in your car at the same time. Do you notice what they do when something isn't selling? They put it in huge bins in the middle of the aisle, so you have to bump into it, with huge markdowns on these items. They are trying to get their money out of something that isn't producing. Look around you and your place, how much stuff do you have lying around that isn't generating money. These things are wealth thieves. Sell the wealth thieves, get your money back out of them and get that money making a return for you.

Two more concepts I would like to cover while we're talking about money. The terms financial and economic may sound the same but are very different. Financial decisions are having the money when you need it, where economic decisions deal with overall profit and such. Here is an example. Let's say that you find an incredible deal, for ten-thousand-dollars a year you can lease a ranch big enough to run a thousand head of mother cows per-year, without feeding any hay. What an incredible deal, right? You know that on this operation your annual cow cost would be quite low. You know you could make an astonishing profit right? Knowing that and committing to the deal is an economic issue. The catch is that you must pre-pay for the next ten years now. So you would need to find a hundred-grand even to begin the deal. Trying to find a way to have the cash precisely when you need it is a financial issue. Think about financial management as managing your money as you go along, and economic management as when we get to the end, and all the dust has settled, did we make money, or lose it?

Feed

I'm going to call all the grass/feed/land issues as feed. Because that what the land grows and what grass is. But even if you are in a confined feeding situation, land still produced the feed you have. So feed management is what we will refer to this as. You need the appropriate feed for the animals, to meet the goals you have for them. In this industry, we are ultimately feeding the world a nutrient dense food source, that we produce from forage, which comes from sunlight. You need adequate nutrition for the animals you are going to own. This doesn't necessarily mean that you have the best feed possible. Production should be secondary to profit. Profit should be first. You can make an animal gain four pounds a day and lose a hundred-dollars per-head. Does that make any sense? When you weigh the cost of everything- perhaps gaining a half-pound a day would have been more economical and you'd have made money- that is why feed management goes hand-in-hand with economic and financial management.

You must never run out of feed (just like you must never run out of money). That seems to go without saying but you'd be surprised at how many people will run themselves out of feed. If they run out of feed it puts them in a situation where they *have* to sell the livestock. When you have to sell you are at the mercy of the market. When you have plenty of feed and money you have a lot of options. You have in your inventory time, when you run out of feed you also run out of time. (Are you beginning to see how feed, time, skills and money are all related?)

Like I mentioned in the last chapter, not every ranch produces the same types of feed at the same times of the year. What forage resource do you naturally have now? What is your climate? In what seasons is there high and low-quality forage available? You can change the resource over time with proper management, but what is out there now? In what form does it come? Is it browse, is it at a high altitude, is it flat lowland native prairie? How any given resource is managed will ultimately determine the production of it. Continuously grazed pastures will deteriorate over time. Unlike continuous grazing, management intensive grazing practices will reverse the deterioration and bring more productivity back into the pasture. The more holistically you can make decisions the better it will all be.

Livestock

First, ask yourself honestly if you should even own any livestock. Could you sell your grass and your skills to someone else who owns cattle, and make the kind of money you are wanting, without having to put your own money at risk by buying livestock? If the answer to that question is no then it would be better to buy livestock for yourself. The next question to ask yourself is what species should I buy? Consider your forage base and storage inventory. If you are purchasing all your feed in condensed form, meaning it all gets trucked in and it's in a bale, or pellet, or whatever, you may consider that feed being too expensive, probably, to be feeding it to brood animals. A brood animal should be working for you, not you working for it. If you have to feed pregnant animals, you are spending more money, and you might be in the wrong business. On the other side of the coin, if all you have is old dried out natural feed out on large acreage, then maybe trying to put a lot of weight on freshly weaned calves or lambs is not the right business. Think about this objectively and be honest with yourself. Next think about some other inventories like your skills, your labor pool, your facilities. Take the time and run each type of business in your mind and see if something might fit a little better. If you are already running a livestock business, what do you have now, and would a different enterprise work better for your situation?

After you've asked yourself what animal you "should" run, now the question becomes what animal are you going to run. We all have things we want to do more than others. So decide what you're going to do. Now figure out what you'll need to be successful.

What things or systems will be essential for your enterprise to succeed?

All of our inventories are interdependent. The success or failure of each of them is directly related to the success or failure of all the others. If you ignore a problem in one area, your entire business will be severely handicapped, or may even fail. There are some that have more priority than others. You can't go broke if you have too much money. You can't go broke if you have too much money and feed. But you can go broke having too much livestock or the wrong livestock and not enough money or feed. So make sure your priorities are in the proper order.

Chapter 4: Play this hand

Other people's opinion of you does not have to become your reality.- Les Brown

Now that you know what your cards are (advantages) now you can play them the best that you can. But life is not one deal of the cards, and that's it. Life is an entire tournament, with a series of deals and how you play them. This chapter is about teaching you the finer rules of the game so you can win in the end. However, don't think of starting your business in terms of a win or loss, take a longer view of it. Even if this hand or a series of hands don't work out, keep playing and learning. We are all running a race for success, but we aren't running against other people, we're running our own race, trying to beat our own best time.

I learned this marketing philosophy from a mentor I had that has since passed away. I spent several days with him learning this philosophy. The first day, he kept repeating the same principles over and over, then we would do some math, or he would tell another example, trying to get me to grasp what he was explaining. After a day and a half of being confused the concepts - all at once it clicked in my brain. I immediately got excited, I turned to him and said "you just made me rich!" he looked right back at me and said, "no, but you can make yourself rich!".

This philosophy will take a paradigm shift on most people's part. But just keep an open mind, and you won't regret it.

Traditional Buy/Sell Cattle Marketing Paradigm

I will buy animals, I will hold them until they gain enough weight or have a calf, after the calf is born and raised or the yearling gains enough weight, I will sell the calves or yearlings, hopefully at a profit. Another way of saying it is, I will hold the animals for months leaving the market to do what it will. I have no control over what the market does. I am a commodity producer which means that I am a price taker. I will take what the market gives me for my product at the time I plan to sell, or when I must sell because I run out of money and/or feed.

Sell/Buy Cattle Marketing Paradigm:

The market will go up and down as it will. I still have no control over the market. I am still a price-taking commodity producer. I cannot change any of this. However what I can control is *when* and *how* I sell the animals, and what I buy back.

The market is going up and down along the timeline of life. At any given time the large cattle buyers in this country are driving the market up for one or multiple classes of cattle, supplying beef for each month of the year to meet with the expected demand. They are filling up as necessary to have a steady supply finishing months from now based on the projected demand. The order today is for only a few weight classes, creating a huge gap in value between the different weight classes. By knowing and understanding what the market is willing to pay for the various classes, a savvy marketer can sell the overvalued animals the buyers want so desperately, and buy the undervalued animals that they don't want.

What few people realize is that these markets are cyclical; the undervalued today will be the overvalued in a month or two. By continually buying the undervalued then selling them the overvalued is proven profitability. No matter if the market as a whole is going up or down there is still a margin between the overvalued and the undervalued. We sell the overvalued and buy the undervalued, capturing that margin in money.

Instead of buying an animal and keeping it until a specified weight or time frame then selling at an unknown price or market condition, we can sell them and buy back the replacement animal to maintain our inventory and capture the margin. By replacing our inventory immediately, we don't open ourselves up to any market risk. The market may go up or down, but by selling and immediately buying the replacement we have no market risk. Marketing this way is a high-cash-flow quick-turnover type business. Instead of turning the inventory once a year like a typical ranch, we can turn the inventory up to six-times a year.

By using this marketing approach (sell/buy vs. buy/sell paradigm), the marketer can control the factors that lead to market risk and financial loss. The best thing about this type of business is the control over so many of the elements that make commodity businesses less reliable. In other industries, the limiting factor is the customer. Those industries spend significant money on customer acquisition/retention. As long as people want to eat, this type of business will survive and thrive. A person's marketing skill and inventory management will decide the measure of their livestock business. This kind of marketing works on all operations. It will work for cow/calf, yearlings, or finishing cattle, and everywhere in-between. Proper marketing doesn't just work in the cattle business, but any commodity business. But it mainly works in any livestock business.

Math Example:

If we Sell a   600# animal for $1.25/# = $750 dollars/hd

And we Buy a 300# replacement for $1.7=$510
There is a three-hundred pound difference divided by
two-hundred-forty dollar a head difference which
equals eighty cents return for every pound of gain
(ROG). If our cost of that gain (COG) is seventy
cents a pound then we have a ten cent per-pound
profit above the profit we have built into our cost of
gain. So ten cents, multiplied by the three-hundred
pound difference is thirty dollars per animal excess
profit, above and beyond the profit that we have built
into your costs. This example is simply here to
illustrate how the math works. Doing this math
procedure is called a "cattle square."

Take a market report go through each weight
class and do the math seeing what the market will
pay you for each class. You will see that some the
market is willing to spend a lot for and others the
market will pay you nothing at all. Doing this market
analysis will tell you what you should be selling and
what you should be buying. You will be able to see
the structure of the current market. Once you've
done one market report, do a different report from a
different market then compare the two.

What/When/How to Market

If you don't own any animals now and are
willing to change your operations between classes of

animals, this is where the biggest opportunities are. However, to stay in one class of animal can be very profitable as well. The following are some guidelines you may consider if you are willing to market between classes.

Breeding Stock: When should we be trading breeding stock? Consider trading your breeding stock when the price of the pound cow plus the price of the calf it will produce are higher than the cost to buy the breeding stock and the cost to run them until another calf is ready to sell. In other words, when you can sell pairs, and buy bred cows as your inventory replacement at a profit. When the cost of calves is below the cost to buy the cow, she is overvalued so don't buy cows. If you can buy the calves for less than the cost of production, you shouldn't have cows, because you can just buy the calves and skip the raising of them.

Stockers: Anytime, because there is always trade opportunities between all the weight classes. From one-thousand pounds clear down to three-hundred pounds there are always weight classes that are in demand, and those that aren't. There is still a margin on something within that range. Occasionally you will have the undervalued animal, and you should keep it until you can sell it and repurchase something undervalued at a profit.

Heavy Feeders/Fat Cattle: anytime, because there is always a constant demand for harvest-ready animals. You cannot always sell fat cattle and repurchase heavy feeders at a profit, so you may have to be willing to buy lighter animals in order for this work all the time. The difference here is that we don't have just to purchase one weight class after we sell fat cattle. We can buy open heifers at one-thousand pounds clear down to a three-hundred-pounder, and there is always a buy somewhere. We can back up as far as necessary. If there isn't a profitable trade, we don't make the deal.

Rules of the Market (If There Are Any…)

When the overall market price is relatively low, a successful marketer can trade pound for pound. This means that you can expand the number of animals you have in inventory.   When the market is high, trades should be made on a head for head basis. Trading head for a head is the opportunity to not put any more money at risk in a high market, that you can guarantee will come crashing down, catching many by surprise. By keeping your cattle numbers the same and just taking your profits, you can pay down debt or expand the operation's natural resources.

When the spread between heifers and steers becomes higher than about twenty cents per-pound, the successful marketer should be buying heifers. There are times when heifers bring a lot less than steers, and other times where there is almost no cost difference, so as the spread increases, more of the inventory should be in heifers, and as the range decreases the marketer has built-in equity building. You will have bought at a bargain at least twenty cents of value that you can re-capture one of these days.

The price of meat is the closest thing to reality that we have. It doesn't matter if we are talking cull cows or fat cattle. The further away from them that we get the more speculation is in the marketplace. What the meat price is today is what beef is worth. What some bred heifer or yearling might be worth is merely speculation. A "fancy" bred heifer may be worth what someone is willing to pay, but an ugly bred heifer or an open heifer is worth what they'll bring on the rail, that's it.

Sale Barn Basics

Sale barns are the ultimate price discovery method known to marketing. Competitive bidding helps us so much in this price taking industry of ours because the buyers are competing to the seller's advantage. However, if you are buying at the sale barn, you want no competition. Buying at a sale barn can be intimidating to some people, and rightly so. The regular buyers may play games with the new guy to see if they can get him to overpay for something.

Buying at the auction is one of the most fun things in the world. It is a very fasted paced environment. You have seconds to inspect everything about the animal in the ring visually. You must make health, soundness, confirmation, and budget (how much you're willing to pay) assessments on the animal in just a few seconds. To learn all of that can sure be a tall order. You will think you made a good buy, then when you get the animal home you realize you paid way too much for it, because maybe it isn't as good as you thought. But if you are willing to dive in and learn that side of the business, it's enjoyable when you start getting the hang of it. Just know what you're willing to pay for each weight class, and don't get caught up in the auction and go over. Don't let the emotion of the moment get to you. Don't think that you have to "win" an auction, that is the first lesson in sale barn buying. Leave the emotion at the door, or you will end up paying for it. The person, you are bidding against might be playing a game with you. If the price gets too high, back down. Let them take that one home. There will be plenty of cattle, they are making more every day, so don't worry. Sometimes the most profitable thing you can do is go home with an empty trailer. That is preferable to paying too much for animals. Do your math, be confident in your numbers, and stick to your plan.

If the lure of quick math and adrenaline aren't your cup of tea, you can do this marketing too. If you don't want to do the bargaining, use an order buyer that you trust. Find someone, and go to see them, spend a little time looking at and talking cattle with them. Don't assume you and they are speaking the same language. You will learn something about the business, and you'll know whether this person is a right fit for you. If it's not a good fit find someone else, and repeat the interview until you see a good fit that you feel comfortable with. By using an order buyer who is already respected and "in the club" of buyers at the auction, the other buyers won't run him near as much as they would run you. So you can let one of them do it. They'll probably get the stock cheaper for you than you could do yourself, in the beginning especially.

Another tip is to give them a budget in dollars per head, not cents per pound. Tell them what animal you're looking for, like a five-hundred pound heifer for no more than seven-hundred dollars per head. Cents have a way of creeping up on you as the end buyer. If they end up buying a five-hundred-fifty-pound animal for a dollar and forty-five cents, it's only a little more weight, and a few more cents, but all at once you are paying almost eight hundred dollars per head. Plus you'll have your buyer's commission added to that. Also if you hire one of these guys, make it clear that if they buy one you don't like, you'll be returning it to them. Rejecting cattle can be a touchy subject, but occasionally you'll get a guy who will buy you junk for high prices and expect you to pay. If this ever happens and he won't take them back, you must pay your bills but fire him immediately. These people are professional cattle buyers, or they should be. They are contracted skilled labor. If you hired any other contractor to do some work for you and they do a lousy job, you wouldn't put up with it either. These guys should be no different. Expect fair treatment and honest business practices. Keep them honest, and everyone else who works for you too.

Also be careful about selling and buying. When you sell some animals, make sure you're at the sale to protect yourself. Be willing to take them home if the other buyers are trying to steal them. Also be careful about buying, even after doing your market research, if you see an undervalued class what you might find is that they are only undervalued because there was only one buyer, and he needed someone else to bid against. Once you join the auction, they won't be undervalued anymore. That is one example of how going home with an empty trailer might be the most profitable decision.

If you're going to do the buying, you don't have to buy them from the auction. Who is selling at the auction anyway? It's your neighbors, so communicate with them about what you're looking for and what you want to pay. If you can buy them out of the country you could have fewer health problems, and you may be able to get them cheaper. But don't be afraid of the auction, it's fun. Just get after it, and enjoy your learning experiences as they come.

Chapter 5: Get Along Little Doggies

Also He blesses them and they multiply greatly, And He does not let their cattle decrease.- Psalm 107:38

It doesn't matter what you buy, or how undervalued it is, if you can't contain it at your place, keep it healthy, and get it loaded back-up to sell it. Learning proper stockmanship is essential *before* you start buying any livestock. The basic stockmanship principles are quite simple, but just like most of the topics in this book, it will take you five minutes to learn the material, but a lifetime to master it. There is no way I can cover all aspects of stockmanship in a single chapter, or even a single book. It would take volumes of literature and flow charts to cover even half of it, but here is an overview of stockmanship.

Stockmanship is the way we interact with animals to get them to go where we want them to. Anytime we are close enough to an animal that it gives us some indication that it knows we are around, we are using stockmanship. Every time an animal takes a step, or turns its head one direction or another, or turns its body, or anything else, it is because of something we did. Try to see what happened before what happened, happened. Read that sentence again. Learn to go back in your mind.

Observe what the animals are doing what did you do just previously. Notice how aggressive you are or how timid, notice your speed, and direction. Also see your frame of mind, are you at war with these animals, and you can't let them beat you, like enemies trying to out-think one another? Feeling like you are on the opposite team isn't how it should be. You should be working with your animals, so that you can do these tasks that must be accomplished together. The term "low-stress" livestock handling is a buzzword these days that doesn't always mean much of anything. We are trying to lower the stress on the animal, but also on the human. Stockmanship is about more than just "low-stress." Its being at the right place at the right time, applying the appropriate pressure at just the right instant and direction to accomplish things with animals.

We eat animals, that's a fact. But they should never feel like they are on the menu today. The reason animals react in ways that we don't like is that they are trying to protect themselves, or they've been trained to be a certain way. If you are driving some cattle along, and one cow keeps quitting the bunch and you have to get her several times, she has learned to get away from pressure by that method. She feels like that is how she needs to escape what is happening. The cattle should not feel threatened, they should be moving because you are moving into their space, not moving out of fear. Have you ever been walking down a narrow hallway when someone is coming at you in the opposite direction? The hall is so tight that your shoulders will touch, and if neither of you gives, neither of you can advance. But that never happens, you both give to each-other, and rarely will your shoulders even touch. Moving with respect, but without fear, is how animals should respond to you. Or, have you noticed how if someone sits on a bench next to someone else, the person who was there first will scoot over just a little bit? That's how it should work. They should move away from you out of slight discomfort, not fear.

I will also say that it isn't all roses getting animals to that point. It also isn't about just loving them, and scratching them behind the ear, and begging them to take a step forward. They should move right out when we pressure, proper stockmanship isn't slow-poke-we-will-get-there-someday. Stockmanship is about appropriate pressure, at the right time, directed at the right place.

With animals all communication is nonverbal. Nonverbal communication is a combination of body movements and energy flow. When I say energy flow, I'm talking about your state of mind. Are you calm or anxious, are you happy or sad, etcetera. All animals can pick up on your mental and emotional state. If you don't think that is right, pay attention to your dog when you are mad, he won't even come around, or if he does he acts differently than when you're in an excited and playful mood. Even humans do this exceptionally well. If your husband/wife is upset, don't you know it immediately, before they have said one word? You can just feel it. Not to be too touchy-feely, after all, we are rough and tough cowboys here, but it is important enough to pay attention to. The emotional well being of your livestock is vital to you, even if you don't know it.

These principles are as old as time, our forefathers inherently know more about it than we do because they spent more time with animals that we do today. The more mechanized and the more technology we use, the farther the gap in communication between livestock and human gets. It all started in the late 1800's with the invention of barbed wire, and the newest thing is robotic milking machines and drones to gather our pastures. I am not against technology, but we are missing out spending time so that we and the animals can learn to understand each other. We must learn to communicate with them in their language. It does no good to speak the English language to them. The old saying is "don't try to teach a pig to sing, you waste your time and annoy the pig."

The Two Steps to Stockmanship: Movement and Direction

There are only two steps to getting animals to do what you want them to do. The first step is to get and maintain good movement in the animals. The second step is having that good movement headed in the direction you desire. I can hear you now "is it that simple?" Well yes and no, yes in that it is that simple but, no at the same time because there are thousands of caveats and nuances that will make it work or not work the way you want.

Good movement is quiet movement. Bad movement is frantic, noisy panicked movement. I don't mean noisy as in auditorily but in the way the animal moves. Watch animals move is it fluid and quiet or is it jerky and noisy? Good movement is not necessarily slow movement. You can trot cows right out with good quiet movement. Good movement attracts other animals to the movement. When there is positive movement in a group of animals going through a pasture, other animals will join from every corner and will follow that movement anywhere. Bad movement repels other animals from wanting to join in. Any frantic, panicked movement from your animals tells you that they feel they are on the menu right this second and if they don't get away their life is over. You should be able to pressure the animal(s), and they respond with respect but without fear. They should move off of your pressure in a quiet and controlled way. You as the director of this symphony can direct it faster or slower or in any direction based on what you're trying to get accomplished.

Getting direction in a herd of animals or a single animal is the same. You want good straight movement. If you have herd movement that is going left and right throughout the herd, it isn't going to help you, because it's not good straight movement. You want the entire herd to be just that, a herd. You want them all of one mind, all headed the same direction. The trick is getting the direction they want to go to be the direction you want them to go. In a herd that is turned well, the movement will not stop, it will keep on trucking in the new direction, but a lousy turn will end all your movement. Pay attention to everything that you do and the response you get from the animals.

Stockmanship Toolbox

The following is a few principles or techniques you may use to help you. These are techniques that will work, but only to the degree that you are doing them correctly for the current situation. Think of them as tools in your toolbox that you can use when you need them.

Using parallel to slow and stop an animal: If an animal is going in a direction that you do not desire, get a fair distance from it, so that you are not making it go faster, and travel parallel to it at the same speed or faster. You can then start the movement in the direction you desire. Make sure you are going parallel or away from the animal, towards the front of the animal. If the animal perceives you are coming towards it in any way, this will speed it up because the pressure is up towards their head. Be moving in a committed and confident way that it will seem to the animal that you are walking to town and just happen to be going next to them. It will feel like it is walking into your pressure. It will want to stop, and let you go to town without them. But if it feels that you are after it, it might not work as easy or quick.

Using parallel to speed up an animal: If you go parallel in the opposite direction as the animal, it will speed up. Get close enough to the animal that you are within its flight zone and move in a committed and positive way. Just like in the previous example of going to town, go right on by and pay no attention to the animal. If you do this, it will see you coming, but you're not coming directly at it so it does not feel threatened, and it can see that it can get by you. It will feel your pressure squeeze into it and will hurry to get past you and go about its business. Going parallel to the movement in the opposite direction is a helpful technique when loading trucks, or in the single file alley behind the squeeze chute, or funneling cattle up steep grades.

The parallel going with and going opposite is the proper way to sort animals. If you move side to side to sort animals, they will not want to come towards you they will, in fact, try to go the other way. If an animal is facing you that you don't want out of the bunch, you don't jump over in front of it, you simply give ground backward until it stops and will return into the bunch quietly. If an animal is looking at you that you want out, take an angle beside it and walk right past it and it will squeeze past your pressure and come right out of the bunch.

Starting Movement

Using perpendicular movement to start herd movement: To start a stopped herd, you go left and right back and forth perpendicular to the direction you want them to go. The speed of the herd is controlled by how flat you are going or how sharp of an angle you are taking towards the animals. If they are moving too fast, you are going at too sharp of an angle and going directly towards them. If they are not moving at all, you are going too flat and going too far. It should take just a few steps to the left and a few to the right a few more to the left, and they should be moving for you. If they are not moving well for you, then sharpen your angle.

Look at the herd, move with committed, positive movement as if you were going to cut about the last 25% of the herd off on one side of the herd. Do not go far enough that you cut it off, but go like you are trying to keep the last few animals back and they will hurry to keep up with the herd. Now, turn to the other side of the herd and do the same thing.

Teaching Livestock to Take Even Pressure

Another technique you might want to employ is teaching the animals to take pressure evenly. If you go towards your animals, do you have a few wilder ones that take off, and also the laziest few that are always at the back of the herd that never move more than a step or two unless you're right there to bring them? This procedure will help you to make a more uniform herd, who will move together when pressured.

Start in a pasture situation, not in a tight corral. Put the animals in the corner. Stay quite a ways away from them. If you go directly and the center or slightly to one side of the bunch when you get so close the wild ones will take off out of there. Adjust your angle so that they can only come out of the herd on one side or the other. Be ready once the first few take off, you will go parallel in the same direction they are going. They will slow and stop and return to the herd. Give them just a minute to regroup, then repeat. After a few times, you'll be getting closer and closer to the herd and more and more animals are leaving at a time. Just keep bringing them back until the entire herd moves as one when you come in to pressure. By bringing them back correctly, this will teach those wild ones that they don't want to be out there by themselves. They would rather be with the herd.

New Animals

Anytime you receive new animals you should work with them so they can accept their new surroundings and the conditions they will have to live under. Teach all new animals to take pressure. If the cattle are walking the fence, then go parallel with the movement until they are all eating, drinking, or laying down. When you drive up to a herd that is in a natural state of mind, at any given time some are eating, some drinking, and some laying down, rarely will they be all bunched up somewhere. You expect to see them all scattered out doing their own thing. If you don't see that, you have a problem that must be addressed, or you will begin to have more significant problems, like sickness or death. If animals are eating drinking and getting proper exercise, they don't get sick and die.

Be careful about taking too much movement out of animals by going parallel with them and stopping all movement day after day. You can take it too far, if they are all laying around most of the time and not exercising themselves it's up to you to see that it's done. They are depressed if all they do is lay around, so work on putting a little movement back into them. Don't do this by chasing them or making them wild. Just move them more. One good thing is to put them in a narrow alleyway and get them to squirt by you a little this will put some life back into them. You don't want them too wild or too depressed. You want good healthy cattle.

For the sake of emphasis, I'll say this again, stockmanship concepts are quite simple and easy to understand but will take a lifetime of learning to get to a level of mastery. Once you think you're getting the hang of this, try something different or do it a different way and you will find that you don't know as much as you think you do. For these animals to work for us like we want, we have to teach them to be that way. Spoiled animals or gentle animals didn't get that way by accident. Every time you are around your animals you are teaching them one way or the other, so make sure you're teaching them the right things.

This overview is exceptionally vague and is just scratching the surface on this topic. If you are going to have any livestock, you have to become a better stockman. I don't care if you have cowboyed your whole life, or you are as green as grass, you need to be a lot better than you are now. Stockmanship is a topic that you must commit to learning more and more every year throughout your career, because you're either getting better or worse, you are never staying at the same level.

Chapter 6: Grinding It Out

"Never give in never never never. In nothing great or small, large or petty. Never give in except to convictions of honor and good sense. Never yield to force, or the overwhelming might of the enemy"-
Winston Churchill

After meeting someone who was a successful, happy rancher, which was opposite of what I thought was possible; after spending as much time absorbing anything I could from him; he started directing me in directions to answers I didn't know I needed. I spent the next ten years or so learning the fine details of successful, sustainable ranching.

I read any book my mentors told me to read. I went to any seminar I could find on alternative or successful ranching. I was exposed to so much good material that it would fill volumes. How much I've retained is not quite as big as I'd like. It's sort of like trying to take a drink out of a fire hose, you get a lot all over you and very little in you. The sheer amount of knowledge one must possess can be completely overwhelming. Which is one reason I keep most any book I might want to reference later, you should see my library! I've learned to love books. I was learning all the doings of successful ranchers. I thought that as long as I did the same things, I would achieve the same results. I was expanding my focus from just ranching to any successful business because I knew that the principles overlap. I read and went to any seminar be it real estate investing, stock trading, ranching anything.

During those years went through several jobs and several part-time businesses. None lasted very long. I couldn't work anywhere very long because I hated working for someone else. I couldn't stick to a company very well because my mind would always be on agriculture. If your mind is not in it, it *can't* succeed.

I buckarooed on several ranches. I learned to ride and rope reasonably well. I worked on my marketing, horsemanship, dogmanship, and stockmanship obsessively. After a full day's work, instead of retiring to the couch with a cold one to fall into a tv coma for the night, I would be doing cattle squares, or watching videos, or practicing something.

When I felt like I'd reached a level of proficiency I thought that I could start my own full-time grazing business. I'd learned by this time some of the ways other people had started ranches from nothing. So I began leasing land and grazing other people's cattle. I always had a full-time job, and did what I could on the side to build my future. Myself, my wife, and our children began a new adventure where they could be more involved. I've never really enjoyed most jobs because you can't take your family to work with you. It's always been amazing to me that most professions require that you spend more of your life with people who you don't choose into your life rather than those close few that you have chosen.

The opportunity came that we could lease a farm that was almost big enough to make a living. I would have to do some outside work to make ends meet but the bulk of my time could be spent at home working for myself. This new life would be great, instead of working full-time for someone else and part-time for me I was now full time for myself and part-time for others. Life was exciting; this was the launching of our new lives and optimism abounded. So we got enough money to operate on for the year and lined some custom graze cattle up. However, optimism without fundamentals will only get you so far. I had spent years learning about livestock and marketing. Grass management and estimation was my weakness, halfway through the grazing season, we were entirely out of grass. With very little money to buy outside feed, the yearlings we took on the gain that year didn't gain anything. The cattle owner sure wasn't happy, and neither were we. You see the only operating money we could secure was from my good old friends and Visa and Mastercard- my friendship with them had a falling out after some missed payments. Times were getting hard, we looked prosperous but weren't. My dream had become a nightmare. Bill collectors were calling at all hours of the day and night making threats of all kinds. Optimism no longer abounded it was more like sheer terror. When you are making decisions from a place of panic, it never ends well. The future looked bleak. I felt like someone who was drowning who could never get a full breath of air.

We had just enough money that one of the options available to us, and the one that we took, was to start a trucking company to subsidize the farm. I could hire someone to watch the farm and cows while I went trucking, and got us out of this mess. I was just living on hope. We went through several ranch hands who sure didn't help our situation. After lots of damage, and dead cattle, our situation looked ten times worse as it did just a few months earlier. We not only owed everyone we owed money to before, but now we owed people close to home too. My reputation in the ranching community was headed in the opposite direction than I wanted. I have always thought of myself and an honest and upstanding person, but from the outside, it sure couldn't have looked like it. I learned how amazingly thin you can stretch a penny.

On the ranch side, things didn't look good, but trucking was doing ok, so my attention got diverted to that 100% because it was the only thing making money. Over the next two years, I made over a million dollars trucking. We built the truck and driver numbers up quite high. Things were going along nicely, we were paying people off as we could, and trying to hang on to the farm. Trucking was paying the way for all of it. Our lease on the land was set to expire in another year, I just wanted to hang on and at least try to be even when it was all over. I knew I couldn't divide my energies if the trucking company was going to succeed. I would have to set aside my ranching thoughts. I had learned earlier in life that if you didn't focus on something, it couldn't work. So the farm sat vacant while I was trucking. My mind had reverted to get rich doing something else for a short time, then I'll have all the money I need to ranch.

The next big lesson to learn was about the risk-to-reward ratio. Having all those trucks running out there all over the country was extremely risky, for the way I was managing the business. At a crucial transition moment, we had some trucks wreck within a few weeks of each other. Fortunately, no human fatalities happened-I'm not sure I could've lived with that. But the cargo of cattle didn't fare too well. Just because you have insurance doesn't mean everything will be ok. Things just got from bad to worse, with insurance costs going up six-fold because of the wrecks we couldn't afford to keep trucking. It started a downward spiral, and because the trucking company was carrying the ranch, it all came crumbling down. When the dust settled, I had a negative net worth of around a quarter million dollars. I was broke; I had drowned. The problems I was facing all snowballed from my lack of grass savvy.

I underestimated the amount of feed that that place would produce and didn't have the money to make it provide more. Then I made terrible decisions that came from a place of fear and panic. I learned some valuable lessons during this time.

My next move was a simple one. I was able to borrow a 46-year-old jeep and spent much time and money working on it to keep it running while I commuted to my new truck driving job. My aspirations were no longer on owning a ranch, I was concerned about keeping my kids fed. My life had transformed from buckaroo to ranch operation owner back down to a truck driver. I felt like the biggest failure. I knew that it was possible to start something from nothing, but I didn't know if I had it in me to do it. I wasn't sure I had what it took to be successful. These days were the darkest point in my life.

Chapter 7: Three Steps to Success

You become what you think about most of the time-
Earl Nightingale

After feeling like the biggest failure in the world, even feeling embarrassed to go out in public. I started learning a different subject. I started delving into some philosophy. I began learning about the "law of attraction". After much time invested into the workings of the "law of attraction", I began to relate it back to my theological studies of earlier in my life. Use of the law of attraction is simply the application of faith. Faith or belief in any particular thing is what makes it turn out as it does. The basics are to decide what you want. As long as it is legal, moral, or ethical, I believe God is ok with you wanting it and achieving it. Next is to begin the journey towards it, and finally, never to giving up. By applying these principles, combined with the belief that what you want is possible, the opportunities to create it in your life will begin to show up.

1. Decide

The first step is to decide what you want. You can wish for a thing, but that isn't the same as a decision. I am not talking about saying "oh yeah sure I'd like to do that." I'm talking about a serious decision. A decision that will sustain you through all of the bumps in the road that you will most definitely encounter. A decision that says "I want this thing and I don't care what gets in my way", "I will accomplish this come hell or high water." A real decision is saying "I'm going to do it, that's it, period." For a decision to be a good one, there must be some emotional commitment and endurance. So the big question you must ask yourself is "why," why do I want to do this thing?

If you don't have the necessary sticking power ,because your "why" doesn't mean enough, you will just have wasted time, energy, and probably money, on something you can foresee won't succeed. You must know and understand yourself. You must know what you will do and what you won't do. You must know what you can do and what you can't do. Don't try to do what you won't do. Don't try to do what you can't do. You will fail.

I would start with an objective "SWOT" analysis. A SWOT analysis is about analyzing your internal strengths and weaknesses, as well as external opportunities and threats. Know your limitations or weaknesses. What precisely is your plan to overcome them. You can hire to your weakness, but be careful. If they are doing a lousy job how will you know? You can work on your weaknesses, but that can take a lifetime before you are perfect in every area. You don't have that much time. You have one life to live, and the clock is ticking. Let's get after it.

2. Start today

The second step to achieving anything is to start right now, today. Your big dream should be huge. The right size dream will take ten lifetimes to achieve. Look at Walt Disney, his dreams still aren't fulfilled. Let's say, for example, that your goal is to start a restaurant chain in every major city in the world, with hundreds of locations. But, today you don't have any locations, or restaurant experience, or any money, or any skills. This goal is so big, that you don't even know where to start. It seems overwhelming, and you fear you'll get bogged down in the details. But the journey of a thousand miles begins with a single step.

Take your giant dream and break it down into smaller steps, baby steps if necessary. Ask yourself what can you do today (now, or fifteen minutes from now, not tomorrow) that will be a baby step from where you are now and the big dream. Maybe that next baby step is downloading an ebook on marketing, or business management, or something.

You decide but do it today. Start now. If you never start, you'll never get there. The sooner you begin the journey, the sooner you'll be there.

If you wait to figure every detail of everything unknown in the future before you start, you'll never start at all. If you were going to drive across the United States and you are waiting for all the lights to be green before you start you would never start, and you would never get there. You see the world different than it is. The way you perceive things is affected by everything you've ever experienced in your life. The dream you have, and the rough plan you have to get there is full of faulty assumptions. What will happen, is you will start on the journey, and a fact will replace of one of those assumptions. Sometimes these facts are small and don't change the plan much, but others change the entire thing. The way you think it will happen, isn't how it will happen. If you are going to start driving cross country you just start going. When you need fuel, you get fuel. When you need to stop, or swerve, or turn, you do, you figure it out as you go along. There are so many unknowns that you can't know all the variables before you start. Just take one baby step today. Then take another one tomorrow. Maybe the first step is just to figure out what some baby steps are. Then do one of them. Success isn't a sprint; it's a marathon. So take a deep breath and just begin, right now today. Earl Nightingale also said -"Success is the progressive realization of a worthy ideal."

3. Never Quit

If I've decided on an accomplishment that I want to achieve, and I've begun the long, arduous journey, and I never give up, I will get there. I might not get there today or tomorrow or this year or next year, but if I never give up, I will get there eventually. If I've decided to chop down a massive tree with a hatchet, I find the tree and begin whacking at it. Even if it takes me days, weeks, or months, if I keep chipping away, at some point the timber will fall. The courage to continue when things seem hopeless is the most crucial part. Quitting when you've come this far is a decision to fail.

As you recall from earlier, when I was 14, I decided that it was impossible for me ever to own a ranch of my own. That was it, when a decision is made it has a finality to it. For a while, I didn't even look for answers- and I wasted that time. It wasn't until I was older that I decided I was going to pursue this dream, no matter what.

To finally get to what you have defined as success won't be easy, but it can happen if you never give up. No matter what happens, no matter how bad it gets, no matter how hopeless it seems or you feel. Keep trying, keep whacking at that tree, and it will come down.

Chapter 8: The Dark Room

Everything we see in the world that was created by a man was first created in his mind- Bob Proctor

Where's the Target?

    Imagine for a minute with me. You find yourself in a dark room, very dark. So dark in fact, that you literally can't even see your hand in front of your face. Not figuratively, but you literally tried and can't see your hand. The floor is hard it feels like maybe it is made of concrete like you are in a warehouse or something. There are no sounds and no visible light. You suddenly feel cold, not because of the temperature in the room, but because you feel alone and slightly concerned. You begin to take some careful steps around and grope at the air, trying to find out if you are all alone in the room or if there is someone or something there. All at once you are startled by someone yelling "FIRE!". You immediately look around for the flames, but you see none. Your sense of smell engages to try to pick up any traces of smoke, but you smell nothing.
    Just as you are about to call out to whoever this human fire alarm is for some clarity on your situation, all the lights come on in a brilliant flash, your pupils

are dilated, and so the sudden light hurts your eyes. As your sight returns, you see that you are in a large warehouse, and just in front of you is a table that is holding a bow and an arrow, and approximately a hundred feet away beyond that is a target. As you scan the room, you see that behind you some distance is a very good friend of yours. You sigh with relief at something familiar. Your friend says "you didn't hit it, you didn't even shoot, why?". You protest right back, "I couldn't see anything." Just then the lights go out again your friend assures you that everything is alright. Just get the bow and arrow and try to hit the target. So you slowly creep forward until you find the table that holds the bow and arrow. You pick it up to aim where you remember the target being, and you hear the same command "FIRE!". You shoot the arrow and it goes flying. You hear the arrow bounce off the floor and go sliding, you know immediately that you've missed the target. You are slightly disappointed but still unsure what this exercise is all about, when the lights come back on. You immediately notice that the target is not where it was the last time that the lights came on, it has moved. You're suddenly more irritated than ever. Your friend is bringing you another arrow, and you ask what this is all about. Your friend says "just hit the target, it's fun." "But it's dark and the target moves, how on earth am I supposed to hit it?" you say in protest.   Your friend gives you a warm and reassuring smile and says "just try again."

Once again the lights go out, and you aim where you last saw the target. The command once again to "fire" arrives and you let it go. Missed, again. With the lights on again you notice once again that the target has moved yet once more. You are frustrated, you feel cheated. You feel like you've been set up to fail. You're entirely ticked off. I mean how can you hit a target that you can't even see?

That is the point exactly. Unless you clearly and precisely have a target to shoot at, you will probably never hit it. You can shoot and shoot and shoot with no positive results. Shooting and missing is how most people go about achieving the goals that float around in their heads. Their mind, which is cluttered with everything we think about from one day to the next is like the dark room. And, as life changes, so do your goals, that is why the target moves.

Every good book on achievement will mention something about goals. Do you think that is a coincidence? It is because anyone who's achieved anything knows that when you write goals down, they become real. It is like writing a contract with yourself. An agreement with yourself that will hold you accountable to the task of getting from where you are to where you want to be. If you write your goals out on paper and have them in your face every day, you can't ignore them as quickly. If where you want to go is consistently in your mind, you almost can't make yourself waste time or money. You'll be driven from within to achieve. You will be able to tap into that never-ending energy source that is deep down inside of us.

Defining Success

The first step to having any success with goal-writing is to define your success. I want you to take some time and think about how you define success. Some people want to be a billionaire, others want to be a millionaire, and yet others' dream is to own their own little ranch with some cows. There is no right or wrong when it comes to dreams. Your dreams are your own. At this stage, I want you to think about the enormous dream, the biggest dream. Don't get hung up on how you will achieve it. Don't spend time thinking about the details. Think only of the largest dream possible. Write that out, put it into words. Whole books have been written on this "think huge" concept, and it is crucial. Just make this dream as big as you can make it. Get immersed in the emotions you'll feel when you've reached your definition of success.

Your belief in what you can achieve is as important as what you want to achieve. What I want you to do next is to get a piece of paper & a pen. Go ahead; I'll wait… Now it's time to get more detailed. On your paper I want you to write a list of ten things that you want in your life that you don't have now. These can be material things like cows, or a truck, or a Rolls Royce, or a new washing machine. The things on this list can also be things you want to achieve, like learn a new language, or become a rancher, or whatever. Don't over-think this, just instinctually write down a list of ten things you want. Go!

Now look at your list. Don't just glance through it, really look at each item on your list. Now I want you to ask yourself this question. Which one(s) on this list do you think you can accomplish within the next six months? Circle or highlight them. These are the goals that you should be focusing on every day. The big dream is important, but it will evolve and change as you evolve and change throughout your life. So just let the big dream be just that an ever-changing daydream of what it could be like someday. But focus on these few items that you believe you can achieve. Do this exercise regularly. Keep motivation tools like this one to move you forward, in front of you all the time. Motivation will be the fuel that will keep you going when things aren't going as you plan.

Take the first few items that you can accomplish. Look at them, and break each one of them down into much smaller steps. What is something you can do today to take one step towards achieving each of them? Then do it. What you've just done is created a plan and a path to follow. Just go to work on it. Work every day towards it and never quit trying and eventually, you'll get there, and after you've achieved one the rest will become much more accessible. Once you get the hang of making and achieving small goals your goals will naturally get more significant. Before you know it, you'll be living the big dream you have for yourself. You must maximize each day to the fullest. Work hard at attaining the small goals, and they will build your dream life.

Chapter 9: Win at the Highest Level

You can have, be or do anything and everything you want- Kevin Trudeau

Mentoring

Successful business of any kind is not an individual sport anymore. Back in the old days to start a ranch all you needed a horse and rope and enough courage to protect what you'd acquired. Starting a livestock business is no longer done that way. Today we live in the information age, and the people with the correct information win the biggest. There is no way you can know everything you need to know to be a winner in business today. The fact is that you need other people. One of the most important people you need is a mentor. The best mentor is someone who has what you want, and who has been where you are. If someone has what you want, but has never been where you are, then you won't be able to relate to them, and they won't be able to help you as much, because they can't relate back to you.

Mentor finding can be a bit tricky. But I believe that when the student is ready, the teacher will appear. I have been very fortunate to have some of the best mentors that money can't buy. The truth is you are smart enough to learn through trial and error. The problem is that you will make a mistake then it will take time to rebound to where you are financially, emotionally, physically, and mentally ready to try again. The result could be that you learn all you need to, but you only have one life to figure this out, and you will run out of time. Find someone who has what you want, and learn from them. This will get you decades ahead of the trial and error method. So, find a mentor. Next, start spending some time with them if you can. A paid internship is probably not going to happen. You may have to move closer to them. You may have to work for free. Do whatever it takes to get in their midst. Do not stalk them or irritate them and end up with a restraining order or in jail. That is taking things too far. Just gently work your way into their lives by any means necessary. Many successful people started as caddies at high-end country clubs. They just started where they could and grew from there. A mentor will be able to see the path you are on and if it needs correction or not.

You don't need a mentor that is a friend to you. You need one who will tell you the hard things you need to hear, not what you want to hear. Someone telling you what you need, not what you want, will require humility on your part, trust that they are genuinely trying to help you. Swallow the bitter pills and learn as you go. A good mentor will change the course of your life, and you will never regret any time you invested. You can be mentored by people online these days. You can even learn the best thinking someone else has done and what they've learned by reading books. Read and re-read biographies and autobiographies of people who have qualities you desire. You never know where some useful information will come from, and they should help keep you motivated as well.

Team Building

With a good mentor guiding you, you will also need other types of help. You will need some professionals like bookkeepers, accountants, lawyers, veterinarians, nutritionists, etc. You might need all of them, but those you do need, you probably won't need them all the time. You just need an inventory of people who you can call on for advice or services when needed. Begin to gather these people into your life. All you need is a good phone number for them, then when the time comes don't be intimidated to contact them. I'm sure they will be happy to help. If they're not, throw their number away and get someone else who is willing to help. Finding the right people to ask is another reason where a mentor is priceless. You can piggyback off of their advisors if they permit.

In the earlier chapter on inventories, we were discussing time. There, in fact, is a way of gaining more time. It is possible is to hire work done that you could otherwise do yourself. An example would be hiring a bookkeeper rather than you investing the time and money to learn bookkeeping, and the hours it will take to do your own books. Another example is you might hire someone to dig the post holes and repair the fence for you for a minimal cost, and that will free your time up to do things you want or need to do. The human resource department of your business is one the most important. Any business is a people business first. Without the proper human resources, you will never have any more time. This time you gain can be used to work on your business instead of in it so much.

Your dream might be a small one person show for your business. Doing all of the work yourself is perfectly fine. I have a few things for you to consider. What if you need or want a vacation or you want to attend some seminar coming up? Or even imagine that you want to go fishing one day, or catch up on some reading. Wouldn't it be great if you had a part-time or occasional help that you've trained to help you when you need? Of course. The other thought is about risk protection. Any personal injury to you in our industry could be quite severe. It could be career-ending for you. Don't spend too much time thinking along these lines but you must contemplate the worst. What if you were in a wheelchair for the rest of your life? Wouldn't it be great if you had some human resources already poised to step up, so your business doesn't have to end? You could still have your business and do all the thinking, but the work would pass to someone else. Unless you have people up and coming all the time, this can never happen. The other truth of it is if you have some help, you can get more done faster. I have a note for those "control freaks" out there - other people *are* capable of doing the work. You are not the only one on the planet who is qualified. If you've ever been around draft teams you know that if you hook two animals together, they don't pull twice the load, they can pull three or four times what one animal can pull.

Chapter 10: Breakthrough

Sir, I have not yet begun to fight!- John Paul Jones

There I was, I had lost everything that I had been working towards my entire life. There was no reason to keep dreaming big dreams. I mean it's impossible, right?

So let's fast forward a few years. Now we are buying a property that we are building a feedlot on. We lease a mountain pasture property that is quite large. We use the marketing principles to run various cattle classes. It all depends on what the market tells us we should buy. We are on our way. We are building wealth one inventory turnover at a time. Though we are still cleaning up some of the financial mess, things are headed in the right direction, and it feels great. I feel accomplished and excited about the future. I have started and been in business for over a year now, and life couldn't be any better.

The details of how I made it are mostly irrelevant to you and your journey. What is essential for you to know is that I made it and you can too. The way I got to where I am won't work for everyone. Each of our paths is different, so I don't want you thinking that my way is the only way. I want to evoke some thought and creativity on your part so that you can carve your own way out of it. I just want to inspire you to get realigned and keep working towards your goal. If you'll decide on a target, get started today, and never quit trying, you will get there also.

The remainder of this chapter is some stories of myself and others who have started from wherever they were and had achieved what they wanted. I have mixed the details of the stories up on purpose. I've also thrown some fiction in to protect the names and places of actual events. My story is intertwined in all of them. I'll leave it up to you to decide how I went about it. But also glean from my friends' stories what might apply to your situation and may help you get down the road of your journey faster.

Work for Equity

I know a person who dreamed of owning a ranch from his youth. My friend "Beau" grew up on his parent's ranch. The problem was that the ranch wasn't big enough to support either his parents or his family. Truth is, if his father didn't keep working his union job he couldn't afford the ranch either. The ranch was a part-time job for both husband and wife. Beau's father was getting older, but still had twenty years or so before he was ready to retire. His parents tried several ways to create value and carve a spot out for the son. Nothing seemed to work. They tried leasing another place and expanding their herd. This strategy turned problematic because the two ranches were quite a ways away from each other, and neither place was big enough to produce enough value. It just didn't work.

But Beau didn't give up. He kept searching, asking himself how could he do it, instead of telling himself that it would never work. One of the father's neighbors had a sizable place. The owner of this place was a widower whose only child had died as a baby. He was getting quite old and slowing down. His ranch was in much disrepair. The widower often talked with neighbors about needing a young person around, but couldn't afford to pay anyone as his place wasn't producing a lot either. The stress of an operation of that size weighed on the widower. Ends barely met, and it became harder each year as his health deteriorated. A plan began to develop in Beau's young mind. He acted on it. He contacted the widower with a proposal. He would come to work for the widower. The widower interrupted the young man and reminded him that he couldn't afford to pay anyone as he was strapped to pay his bills. Beau smiled at the widower and explained his idea. The widower loved the idea it was a win-win for everyone.

The basic agreement they came up with was that he would come to work for the widower for equity, not money. He would work for the widower part-time in the beginning then it would turn full time later. Beau went to work immediately to correct all the deferred maintenance that was required to bring this place back to life. When it came payday however instead of a check, he got one cow per month. Month after month, this went on for a few years. Beau would brand the cow with his iron, as his cow. If he left, he took his cow with him. He also got anything his cow produced. He paid the widower a grazing charge for each animal he ran on the widower's ranch. With a decreased workload the widower's health began to improve.   Over time Beau owned all the cattle and was in essence leasing the ranch from the widower. You see now the widower now owned a ranch that could be sold for more money because it had been fixed up by the young man. The widower gained monthly cash flow, and Beau earned sweat equity.

At this point, they made another arrangement for the land. They agreed to a type of reverse mortgage. So instead of paying a lease payment to the widower, Beau would start making a land payment. He was building equity again. Years went by again and as the widower's health began to deteriorate again. At the time that the widower passed away the young man got a conventional loan for the remaining balance owed on the ranch, of which he already had considerable equity in. The loan amount paid the heirs of the widower as was stated in their contracted agreement.

The young man was willing not to own it all today, and was able to work for sweat equity which paid him much better than a good job ever would've. He had to do things the way the widower wanted them done whether he agreed or not. Beau also really helped the widower out. The widower was in a tight position; he owned some assets that were going down in value every day. He couldn't attend all the work that was required to keep a place of that size up. The widower also gained his dream of having a "son" to pass his place on to. The widower gained monthly cash flow until the end of his life. Beau went on to buy other neighbors' places and also is buying his father out at this time. He's started from basically nothing and created a place for himself and his family. He is a full-time rancher and loves it.

Get Rich First

Another person I now also loved the idea of ranching. I mean what small boy doesn't want to grow up to be a cowboy someday? Almost all of them right? This boy was no different, but his strategy was very different from the young man who worked for equity. He inherently knew it would take a truckload of money to get started.

"James" went to college then on to law school. He started a practice in a large city. He hated the city, he continually dreamed of the time that he would be able to buy his place in the country. Over the course of about ten years, he built his practice to quite a large, successful size. Because of his status and education, he knew how to get things done. When he was financially stable enough and was ready to, he got a mortgage on a small ranch across the state from the large city where he resided and worked. He did this for several reasons; he knew that if the ranch started taking too much time from the law practice, his law practice would suffer so he bought someplace that he couldn't attend to after work. He also knew that he lacked the necessary skills to ranch correctly, he'd spent his time and energy practicing lawyering not cowboying, so he hired a competent manager who worked the ranch for him. He had become an absentee owner, it was great he could go on long weekends to his ranch and help out. He loved going there and working his place fixing the fence and working cattle. He became more and more reluctant to head back to the city to earn the money that was funding this side business. But he did it anyway, he was diligent and reaped the benefits.

Over time he bought a few more places and at the time of his retirement he owned several ranches totaling about a 600 mother cow outfit. The other cool thing about this story is his son followed in his footprints. As the father retired from the law business, the son had taken the practice over. The son also loved to come to the ranches that his father had built. The son worked the practice well and grew its size. He added other ranches to the operation and had just about doubled the size of it. He took the head start his father gave him and he grew it into something quite impressive. The father has now passed away, and the son has retired from the law practice and is running the ranch full time. They've kept a manager and other workers around the whole time. They just get to show up and do the fun stuff. Not a bad plan.

Start Small and Don't Quit Your Day Job

The third story I have for you is yet another strategy of achieving the same end of ranching. This story starts where a young lady grows up in the heartland of America in Small Town, USA. Her family runs an operation of some cows and some row crops. Just a basic generic family farm upbringing. "June" graduated high school, then started attending the state university in agribusiness. She's going right along achieving good grades when she gets exposed to some of the same teachers and philosophies I was during college.

A drastic change happened, she dropped out of college to pursue her real dream. She began working in a feedlot as a pen rider. She saved her money until she had a small bankroll so she could begin buying her own cattle. She was able to save six-thousand dollars. Six grand wouldn't buy a lot of cattle, but it was a start. She leased a place big enough for her herd. She kept working at the feedlot and began to buy cattle at the auction for one of the feedlot customers. She also started selling feed supplements to ranchers. Between her cattle buying and selling and her supplement business, she was able to understand the ranchers' needs. She got to see many operations and how they functioned. What was good and was working, and what wasn't working, on their operations. She got so concerned about making her customers money she learned what she needed in her operation to get further ahead faster. As she earned money, she would buy one more animal. The end was inevitable, she was using correct principles to market her animals properly, and her herd and equity grew. After several years of working for someone else while building her business part-time, she was able to quit the feedlot and work for herself. She just kept going one step at a time. She just put one foot in front of the other. She built it one brick at a time. She started with six thousand dollars, and over the course of twenty years, her net worth is over a million dollars today doing nothing more than working at it one penny at a time.

So her story is, she started working for wages. Then she started buying her cattle and just kept building. She traded the job for small wages for her supplement and cattle buying business. She finished off by having her own sizable operation. She still buys a few cattle for her close friends. But how great it must feel to have complete control over her future.

These are real stories of real people who started with basically nothing, no inheritance, no lottery winning, just hard work towards their goal. My story is intertwined in all three. I'm not setting myself out as the example, but instead to implant in your mind that it's possible.

Other Strategies

Like we stated earlier, real estate is not valued based solely upon is production level. Production is a part of the equation, but it is only a part. One strategy to consider is leasing your land base. Leasing is a before-tax cost, where land payments are an after-tax investment. By leasing the land, you can pay for the production of the property. You don't need to own it to have the benefit from it. Sometimes I'm asked if isn't it better to be paying a payment on your own place, than making the payment for someone else to own. Making a land payment for yourself is a very valid point, and this is my response. If you are in a situation to buy the needed land, and in your part of the country, lease rates are high enough that purchasing the land makes sense, you should by the land. If you can lease the production off the land for less than the land payment would be to purchase it then consider leasing, then as your financial situation improves you may want to purchase some real estate and lease it from yourself to help with your ever-evolving tax and financial situation.

Leasing does not have to apply to just the real estate. I know several people who have leased equipment, or even the cattle themselves. Just make sure you do your homework, and you know what you're getting yourself in to.

Another option is to run your livestock with someone else who is already doing what you want to. You will pay a set amount per month or year and get to grow your business while learning important skills. You can be an investor in another operation if you wish. That might be the best fit for you. Or you could just buy stocker or feeder cattle and put them in a custom feeding yard. You can be in the cattle business without ever owning or leasing one acre of land.

People talk about how hard it is today to get started in ranching, that it's impossible. The truth is that it isn't any harder today than it was hundreds of years ago. Start with whatever you have and maximize it to get to where you want to be. The principles of achievement have been the same forever. I know there are countless stories of those who've achieved what they've started out towards. These three are only a few of them. These principles don't just apply the livestock business, I sincerely hope that this book will add value and encouragement and maybe even some direction to anyone trying to achieve anything. The rules of the game might change because we live in a very different time now. We have some advantages that our forefathers never had, but we also have some unique challenges that they never even dreamed of facing. Don't use these challenges as a reason to blame for you not achieving your dreams. Take responsibility for you and your achievements, or the lack thereof, whichever the case is. I sincerely hope that this chapter has made you think of some options in your own life, so you can make your dreams come true. Your journey will look very different from any of these stories. It will be a unique one-of-a-kind story that only you'll be able to tell. I hope you'll look me up and share it with me. The advantages and challenges you face are unique only to you. If it's going to happen, you're going to have to do it. So commit today, start today, and never quit.

Resources

Ranch Mastery Course

If you liked this book but want more detailed training on each of the topics and much more visit

www.myranchfromscratch.com

My Favorite Books and Periodicals

Ranching

Stockman Grass Farmer Magazine edited by Joel Salatin
Stockmanship Journal edited by Whit Hibbard
"The Cattle King" by Edward Steadwell
"I Made a Lot of Tracks" by Phil Stadtler
"Time to Change" by Chip Hines
"How to Not go Broke Ranching: Things I Learned the Hard Way in Fifty Years of Ranching" by Walt Davis
"Knowledge Rich Ranching" by Allan Nation
"Land, Livestock and Life: A Grazier's Guide to Finance" by Allan Nation
"No Risk Ranching: Custom Grazing on Leased Land" by Greg Judy

"Management-intensive Grazing: The Grassroots of Grass Farming" by Jim Gerrish

Success, Business and Finance

"The Seven Habits of Highly Effective People" by Stephen Covey
"How to Win Friends and Influence People" by Dale Carnegie
"Think and Grow Rich: or Men and Women who Resent Poverty" by Napoleon Hill
"The Slight Edge: Secret to a Successful Life" by Jeff Olson
"Rich Dad Poor Dad: What The Rich Teach Their Kids About Money - That the Poor and Middle Class Do Not!" by Robert Kiyosaki
"The One Thing: The Surprisingly Simple Truth Behind Extraordinary Results" by Gary Keller
"The E-Myth Revisited: Why Most Small Businesses Don't Work and What to Do About It" by Michael Gerber
"The Game of Work: How to Enjoy Work As Much As Play" by Charles Coonradt

98789579R00059

Made in the USA
Columbia, SC
02 July 2018